Maggy's Flower

by Alex Gonzalez
illustrated by Shawn McManus

Practice Decodable 75

Mc Graw Hill Education

Bothell, WA • Chicago, IL • Columbus, OH • New York, NY

MHEonline.com

Send all inquiries to:
McGraw-Hill Education
8787 Orion Place
Columbus, OH 43240

ISBN: 978-0-02-144744-2
MHID: 0-02-144744-6

Printed in the United States of America.

7 8 9 CTM 23

Maggy is a plain brown cow. When Maggy is happy, she likes to plow.

Maggy is a big and powerful cow. She is the most powerful cow in town.

Maggy plows and plows. The farmer's pals are amazed at how well Maggy plows.

Maggy sees a little flower. She stops her plow. Maggy frowns and scowls. She needs that flower!

Maggy will not plow. The farmer tries to get Maggy to plow. Maggy just stares at the flower.

Maggy is allowed to keep her flower. The flower makes Maggy happy. And, when Maggy is happy, she plows.